LEO HOROSCOPE 2023

Your essential guide to love, money, happiness and using moon magic!

Hi Guys,

A warm welcome to all my regular readers and a special hello to all new readers. I aim to provide a comprehensive insight into 2023 with spiritual, psychological insight, and down to earth common sense advice.

Every year when I write these books I just cannot believe how fast the year has gone, and that it's once again time to write and publish the series for the next year.

As many of you know, I've been producing these books since 2014, and boy has the world changed since then and 2023 will be a year of unprecedented change in world terms, that's why I've decided to also do an Astrology book of World predictions which include predictions for countries and certain leaders, because I feel that we need to be forwarded and for armed.

It's important to remember that no matter what is happening in the outside world, we all have our lives to live and karma to resolve and we must enjoy our own unique journey. Remember, we are all meant to be here at this very time, to experience what we are experiencing and we should never underestimate our own power and ability to thrive and make a difference.

Yes, we are all at different points along our own personal journey, but what I want to do with these books is encourage you all to understand your own creativity, power and never to underestimate yourself, to feel lost all to lose a sense of purpose. We are all here for a reason and we all have a valuable contribution to make in different ways, and hopefully my annual books have inspired you to understand your purpose and connect with some inspiration.

Fortunately the Saturn Square Uranus that was happening between

Saturn in Aquarius and Uranus in Taurus is now done and dusted, which is a good thing because that was creating an enormous amount of tension within all of us, because the energies of Saturn and Uranus are so different. However, what we have coming this year is Pluto moving into Aquarius, and every time Pluto has changed signs there have been dramatic events worldwide that have changed history: it could be the birth of new countries, technological changes, conflict, economic shifts, innovations and the advent of new philosophies or political systems. So we should all be ready to embrace change with an open mind and we should remember not to be overly concerned with things that we are not able to change, because what we all can change is our attitude and it's always better to be optimistic and proactive.

I've often seen in my career as an astrologer that astrology works best for people who make plans, who act on those plans, who motivate themselves and who don't wait around for things to happen. Good things happen when we take chances, when we get up and seize opportunities or even just envisage then, very little happens we stick to comfort zones, resist change and hang onto the past for dear life, irrespective of the planets.

I always believe that it's important to understand our roots, to know where we come from and how our experiences have shaped us and given us wisdom. Our cumulative heritage is always important, but we can't live in the past, things are changing and we have to keep moving along and adapting, and using our wits and innate dynamic energy to thrive.

Love Lisa

Is this a good year for Leo?

This year the positions of both Jupiter and Pluto are excellent for your self-development, for positive thinking and for rewiring your brain for both success and also achievement in terms of relationships.

This year is quite a powerful and transformative one for Leo and the potential of Jupiter conjunct North node in Taurus is exciting for both romantic opportunities and understanding your true potential. This is an excellent time for you to break habits, get over mental blocks and get in a good mindset for the future.

This is also a good time for you to redefine or reframe the past in a more positive way.

As the planet Pluto begins to move out of Capricorn and into Aquarius, you feel a burden has been lifted and whatever age you are at, you feel you can start with a new slate and you don't have to be bound by the events of the past, no matter how disappointing or no matter how much angst is attached to that.

You tend to be very successful in both business and your personal relationships simply because you display a lot of empathy and tolerance, and you are able to work with people with a better understanding of their priorities, their background and their values and he's far more inclusive of their needs.

Often Leo is known as an individualist, you can be quite competitive and you're not always a team player but in 2023 you understand that the sum of the parts is greater than the whole, and that through incorporating factors like the ideas and the emotional impact to those closest you, the whole package is that much more sweet and successful.

The year starts with Jupiter entering Aries, and that is an excellent appetizer for the year ahead as your creative potential is enormous. This is a time when you could accomplish a great deal and is not deterred by things that would normally seem quite difficult. The energies of the beginning of the year generate self-confidence and therefore you're going to hit the ground running.

If you have been suffering ill health, anxiety or have been trying to recuperate, the beginning of the year will see a burst of good health and a feeling of well-being returns which will permeate your body allowing the energy to flow through your chakras, and good health will be generated from within.

Your Star is Rising

Jupiter in Taurus later in the year indicates your professional and public life coming to focus and this is a marvelous time for recognition, reward and success. It's also a great period for leadership both in a business and community sense. You can be very influential and you have enormous power to change minds and motivate people.

In a way this positive publicity can be quite testing, because often your more personal and intimate life is brought into the public sphere, however, luckily with Leo this is not always as much of a challenge as it is with water signs. You will feel quite self-protective towards family members, so in some cases you will think long and hard about new avenues in your career bearing in mind the impact they have on the family life and personal matters.

Positively Charged

The important thing for Leo to remember this year is that everything starts with positivity, so all emotional and physical healing begins with an attitude of being future orientated, being philosophical as well as holistic, and that means understanding the lessons of life and valuing those lessons, rather than being critical of your failures or envious if other's experiences.

Embracing your Cullinan Diamond

It's time for Leo to re embrace yourself as a unique individual with a unique destiny. It's important for you to establish your own priorities, values and mission statement which gives life and vitality to your existence, rather than trying to compete with others and compete on their terms by doing things that may not have any innate value to you.

What's your mission statement?

The first task for Leo this year, as I mentioned in the introduction, is to come up with your mission statement. You have to redefine what it means to be YOU, what is most important to you and what mark does you want to make on the world. Once you have a clear idea of your mission, this gives your life so much more value within that context, and you no longer finds the need for disappointment and frustration as you can understand that you're doing something that no one else can do and you're doing it in your own inimitable way.

I think Frank Sinatra's 'I did it my way' should be a good theme tune to focus your mind from the beginning of this year on your individuality, and therefore to see your whole life as an expression of that. Understanding your destiny in this way helps you approach your divine purpose.

Changing the Script

It's important for Leo to think of all the things in your life that are illusory and deceptive, often we create narratives in our head that become chains that bonds us, but these are only narratives and we have created them, and we can break them. In 2023 you need to think about this and the beginning of the year is ideal for a period of study into psychology, or even some form of counselling can be an excellent way of resetting your mind for success in love relationships and business relationships.

The Lighthouse

Leo get a great deal of satisfaction from sharing knowledge with others. Any activity that involves teaching, presenting, imparting knowledge or providing insight to people that will inspire them is particularly enjoyable for you.

Leo likes to be listened to, indeed one could say you like the sound of your own voice, and you're a naturally entertaining, but this can all be combined into something that is not only great for your career but very fulfilling for you if done on a voluntary or part-time basis as well. So the more you can impart skills, help others gain knowledge, spread information etc. the more satisfied you feel and this contributes to a growing sense of self-confidence and of value. This year Leo is really understanding the value and respect you have within society and therefore you begins to value yourself more and this put you in a much better situation in relationships.

Healing the heart

Leo can often become damaged by things that have happened to you in your life, you take situations and events to heart and finds it very difficult to say 'who cares, water off a duck's back' and to move on.

Yes externally you look tough as you are quite courageous and have a sunny demeanor, but often you carry scars that are very slow to heal, and this can lead to you losing self-respect and sometimes being a little bit of a walk over in relationships. So this year regaining self-respect is very important to you as it helps you restore balance in relationships and take your power back.

Putting self-respect at the center of your life

How do you gain that self-respect again? You have to do things that create satisfaction and value, so that means you have to get rid of all the activities or the habits that drain your energy, drain your money and are only superficially satisfying without creating something substantial that you can feel proud of or enjoy to the max.

Tapping into the Uranus Electricity

Uranus continues to be in Taurus and it's very important for Leo to ask yourself where you are feeling stuck or restricted. You could be in this frame of mind where you may believe that if you go along with control, if you submit to external forces eventually things will turn around and you will win the day, but very often you're building your own prison by cooperating with these forces and this can lead you despair and also hopelessness.

You need to be able to recognize where feelings of despair or pessimism have actually arisen from your own behavior i.e. in not putting your foot down and in going along with things when you could have easily said no. You should no longer go along with things that feel wrong or go against the grain as that's always no win for you.

Knowing when fear interferes with your true calling

Often the things you fear most never happen, but those fears create a hold over you, preventing you from leading an fulfilling life. So while Jupiter is an Aries, it's essential for you to be courageous, to smash through those fears and to take a few risks. When I say taking a few risks, I don't mean driving like a maniac in the car or skydiving, I just mean taking a risk to do something that you would normally be scared to do, perhaps because it might jeopardize a friendship, a relationship or even your reputation. You should never be scared to jeopardize a superficial value.

Jumping in the deep end

There is a sense this year that you need to jump in the deep end, you need to do it now before you develop cold feet or gives yourself too many negatives. You have to understand in what way, and why you feel restrained and then you need to abandon those restraints and jump in, as Elvis sang, 'Wise men say only fools rush in' however in 2023 for Leo it's often opportune to rush in.

Getting the monkey off your back

This is an excellent year for Leo beginning the process of crushing any addictions or codependent behavior which you endure in your life: these can be substance dependency, sometimes it can be unhealthy relationships, hoarding and sentimentality as you can begin to recognize these and you have the willpower to begin to stamp them out and break free of them.

What's around the corner?

There will continue to be surprise events, some upheaval and cultural change affecting your chosen career. It's highly likely that

Leo will again be looking at the career sphere and having a totally renewed perspective on what is possible and what you would like to do. If you have been in any career where you are at your wits end or feel that you can no longer generate enough income, this year with Jupiter moving into Taurus, you should see a great deal of impetus for creating opportunities, for striking out independently and for exploring again your possibilities without limiting yourself by obsession with what has gone before.

It's no use in feeling trapped in a job simply because you feel that the job security, the financial rewards or the prestige are worth it, because things are changing in your world, and going forward those things may no longer have value anyway, so they are worth abandoning sooner rather than later.

The great wheel of fortune

Events in the wider economic world continue to produce pressures in terms of how you can conduct your business, whether you become self-employed or the kind of ambitions you set for yourself, but at the same time, Leo being a very creative and audacious character can find unique opportunities and also some fantastic opportunities to shrine, to lead etc.

Very often you can be a beacon of hope to others and you often do this through education, as I mentioned before, and inspiring others. So there may be many new roles coming about, things you can't anticipate now, or hadn't thought about before, but the political changes are creating these openings which will enable you to actually find some much needed satisfaction.

Redrawing the rainbow

In early January Mars turns direct in Gemini and this is fantastic time for Leo because it superchargers the amount of impetus you feel to pursue hopes and dreams. So this is certainly a year for you to start reigniting any inspirational ideas you have for your life. Indeed you should reach for the stars, you should think big and you should start believing in the potential of your life again and believing in your right to have fun and reward.

The friendship factor

At the beginning of the year, networking can be a key way to help you gain confidence in a new field or restore confidence. Joining professional bodies or joining groups where you can go to meetings for the purpose of business and corporate networking can be a very good option.

You really enjoy brainstorming, you love being surrounded by strangers and eclectic groups of people with whom you can hobnob and exchange ideas.

Getting in the know

The first part of the year is fantastic for you gathering information, hearing a little bit of trade gossip, listening to the grapevine and getting the gist of what is going on.

In order for Leo to be successful at the start of the year, you can't think that you can go it alone and you have to surround yourself with people who have experience and expertise, and who can answer your questions or whom you can observe and learn from to make sure that you head in the right direction from the start.

Hitting the ground running

The first part of the year sees you rather energized, but it's often important for you to suppress your competitive and ego needs when it comes to group situations or you can arouse conflict situations and lock horns with people, which can negate the benefit that those people can give you. So it's important for you to take a step back and to get your feet under the table, before you start expressing yourself too powerfully, otherwise you miss an opportunity to really learn.

Health and well-being

In terms of health, physical activity like athletics is particularly good for you and joining groups of people who enjoy sports can inspire you to stick with new fitness routines, and to make the most of the increasing levels of strength, energy and health you're feeling.

You need strong gratification from other people particularly at the beginning of the year, and also with Venus retrograde in Leo, and therefore you're likely to bond very quickly with new people you meet, which means strong platonic friendships can arise. However you can also develop friendships which have a great potential to lead to romance, so there's a lot of benefits for you getting involved with new groups of people, new organizations or even political groups, because it fires up your imagination and gives you courage you to get into better routines regarding exercise, and it's a wonderful place to meet like-minded people and to establish good friendships and romantic relationships.

Traveling in a fried out combi

The beginning part of the year is also great time for you to travel in a group of people, so you may decide to take a trip without knowing exactly who is going to be travelling with you. This can be quite an exciting and stimulating thing for you to do, and also a good way to meet people. Often when one is travelling with others that you already know, one is more closed to 'the other ' but if one travels alone or volunteers to travel in a group of people they don't know one tends to be more open to new experiences.

Staring in the looking glass

Venus retrograde in Leo during the height of the summer months in the Northern hemisphere is an excellent time for Leo to work on yourself, to work on your values, your self-esteem and personal growth. The ideal way for you to repair and restore relationships is by you going inside yourself and fixing what's broken. So you need to practice self-love and you may also have to engage in some meditation to help you with forgiveness and letting go. Often Leo gets into the mode of licking wounds, but there's only so long that suffices before it just leads into a negative cycle.

Leo can often be quite proud and you are the center of your universe therefore you are very focused on how things affect you, whereas if you take a step back and understand other people's needs and problems, it may help you to come up with a more balanced approach to your relationships. It's also great for you to take a step back and stop projecting - Leo are terrible for seeing threats on the outside and then wanting to go up against them, rather than understanding that some of those threats emanate from your own behavior patterns.

Healing is coming home

During the early months and the Venus retrograde you can actually obtain a lot of healing and satisfaction by understanding that the choices you have made, you made for a reason and very often you are where you are because you made choices because of your a value system. If you compare yourself to others, you're comparing yourself to people who have different values, but if you understand what your own values and priorities are and what makes you most happy deep down, then you may understand and come to terms with some of the choices you have made and therefore you can be more positive about those choices, and that can help you to make more informed choices going forward. Often if you're unhappy in your life, it's to do with the fact that your innate values have led you to make choices which don't have the anticipated outcome, and now you must figure out how to get the outcome you want by making choices that are more likely to fulfill for your most deepest held needs.

Appreciation

Your closest relationships go through a period of rebalancing and clarity, there are greater levels of appreciation and a need to reawaken the understanding of what a partner brings into your life, and how important those deep, consistent and strong bonds are. If you are very unhappy in a relationship, this is certainly a year to give it one more try, marriage counselling and advice from others could help you gain a perspective as long as it's professional advice.

Patience in relationships is very important, you cannot afford to be pushy or gung ho, this is a time to be delicate and to be more cognizant of the deeper issues at play. I mentioned that psychology is very important this year and so Leo needs to continue to work on yourself, understand yourself better and that could be achieved through reading and definitely via contact with different people who are possibly less inclined to self-censor. Thus good advice often comes from total strangers rather than from people you knows, because people you knows probably know you too well to be totally honest with you.

Reach out for the healing hands

This year Jupiter will be sextiling Saturn which is in your seventh Solar house. Now because Saturn has been in Aquarius for the last 2 1/2 years, there have been challenges and difficulties for Leo to deal with in your closest relationships. Some relationships have not stood the test of time and may have broken up and other relationships may now require a period of healing. However the Jupiter sextile can certainly help restore trust and affection in relationships that have been hampered by bad feeling, conflict or difficulty in the last few years.

So even if Leo has been struggling to find balance, to get your needs met or to have effective communication in your marriage or long-term relationship, Jupiter should ease these problems and bring back a feeling of fun, easy living and happiness to the relationship, and you should be able to have a few good laughs as humor returns. Jupiter's bonhomie should help you guys to settle your differences draw a line under everything and get ready to move on.

Legal eagle

During this year, it is very important time for Leo to work constructively on any legal problems. If you have an ongoing dispute with someone, you now have to work extra hard at mediation or legal recourse to settle these things once and for all. If there's any problem you are having and you haven't employed a lawyer, now is the time to get legal advice. It's no good for you to speak to friends and lay people, you must get the proper advice and this is the route to fast resolution of these problems.

Are wedding bells ringing?

This is a good year for Leo to get married or engaged. If you have been in a long term relationship and you guys have been talking about whether you should get married, now is the time to commit to each other.

Leo is stronger in a partnership, you enjoy the validity and the gratification being a partnership gives you. Despite you being an individualist, you actually like being a team player in marriage and marriage brings out a good side to you, so you guys shouldn't hesitate, if you've been together a long time, maybe now is the time to pop the question and commit.

Karma Chameleon

The planet Jupiter, which rules your solar house of romance, will be squaring Pluto a few times this year and Jupiter will also be in Taurus, this means you can be drawn into very intense karmic relationships and relationships can happen quite suddenly and inexplicably taking you by surprise.

In some cases you begins to feel romantically attached to someone who you have known a long time and has not previously had feelings for, so sometimes strong romantic feelings erupt at a time and place, or with a person, which takes you by total surprise, but this can lead to a strangely satisfying relationship.

Total eclipse of the heart

This year in April the solar eclipse is square Pluto just before it enters Aquarius, and this year Saturn will enter Pisces which is particularly significant in terms of its psychological effect on Leo.

It's time for you to acknowledge the hidden forces of negativity that keep you in check and that possibly keep leading you down blind alleys. You should also contemplate any problems, both in relationships or other aspects of your life, where you need to own your contribution rather than to identify outside sources to demonize.

Your own subversive hidden forces should not be projected onto outside world, you must rather look within your own thought patterns or habitual behaviors for suspects.

Taking control means taking back power

It's very important for you to arrest those behaviors which create negativity and pessimism in your world. These habitual patterns could be time wasting, obsessions (particularly with social media), negative thoughts or it can be negative psychological approaches like poor dietary habits or avoidance strategies.

Often by taking control of a small 'fear factor' in your life -and what I mean by 'fear factor' is anything you avoid to reduce anxiety - it helps build inner resolve. Thus if you tackles something (and it doesn't have to be huge) which normally causes you anxiety, and you begin to get used to tackling that without the same trepidation, then the more power you feel entering your soul and thus a small thing can actually lead to a significant boost in empowerment.

The great thing about this year, is Leo can potentially feel power entering your life, this is the power to control your destiny, to make your way in the world and to have dominion over your fate rather than feeling a victim of it!

Bones of contention

In new relationships competitiveness, jealousy and games are often rife because there's an element of you and new partner being wrong footed and thus insecure. A new relationship can get off to a tricky start or a feeling that the relationship isn't quite right, you guys are this both very insecure and thus you are more likely to exhibit possessive behavior towards each other.

It's quite important for Leo to get rid of preconceived ideas, because in reality, at the heart of this jealousy and possessiveness is this idea that your relationships is somehow wrong, a bad fit or inappropriate, but where are these ideas coming from? Are they coming from your friends, society or your parents? You guys have to be able to see the relationship for the beauty that it is, without judging it on superficial characteristics, because the more you do so, the more you both feel insecure and thus the base instincts come to the fore.

Getting hot and bothered

Leo is really turned on by partners who are sassy, passionate and have a large appetite for life, however these flamboyant characters are quite high maintenance and can be energy vampires, so the charade of dating can be quite exhausting, which means it's best to take it in short spells rather than to live in each other's pockets, which would drive you both round the bend.

So Leo shouldn't be concerned if in your romantic relationships you are seeing a lot of someone and then suddenly not seeing them for a few weeks, because that can work a lot better than seeing each other continually, simply because relationship themes this year tend to be occasionally frustrating, a little contentious, very passionate and but quite exciting all the same.

Even though relationships are exciting, you guys can have too much of a good thing and you can end up feeling drained snapping it each other or having quite dramatic blowouts, that's why you guys need to incorporate intense periods together with periods where you back off each other and have time to calm down, to rationalize and to be a little bit more objective.

The risk factors

Leo needs to be careful of getting into a relationship with a partner who almost encourages risky or obsessive behavior. You need to take a step back so you can be more objective, because often the relationship is very much within the heat of the moment all the time, and you become extremely emotional and objectively goes out the window, and you can end up making bad decisions in all aspects of your life simply because of the relationship driving up your adrenaline constantly.

Money and Finances

This year Mercury is retrograde in the earth signs: Taurus, Capricorn and Virgo, and these represent your Solar houses of money, work and career. This means that you have to be flexible, open-minded and willing to backtrack in all these areas. So when it comes to money, finance and negotiating pay packages or benefits within work, it's important for you to take a long-term approach, and sometimes you have to allow time for things to work their way through. There's no point in being impatient, and sometimes you have to give things a rethink.

Negotiating with other people can be filled with pitfalls and so you need to have multiple strategies and levels of attack. In terms of earning money, it is always important to have a plan A, B and C, and to quickly get back to the drawing board when things are not going your way. Remember don't flog dead horses, when it comes to money, stay alert for new information that could be pivotal. Don't be stubborn and don't just stick with the plan because you put the work in as things are changing fast, so you need to keep your eye on political developments, legal changes and even changes in a governments, because these can throw your plans into disarray, and you may have to reconsider.

If you are flexible, do your research, investigate well and remain open-minded, this can be an excellent time for new investment schemes, for problem-solving and for finding some very interesting and lucrative new avenues to earn money in.

Hometalk

In terms of family life or property, this could be the year when everything changes. So if there's been a long-term problem that's been plaguing you for a decade or more, this may be the year you finally make a breakthrough or something changes which allows you to deal with the problem once and for all.

It's very important to settle family matters, if there are any outstanding issues or disputes, bring them to an end, preferably amicably, but if not amicably bring them to an end anyway because it's time to open a new chapter.

Moving home is most likely a topic that will be up for discussion, it may be that you and your partner are considering a radical move that will fit in with a major lifestyle change, and so while a move now is a definitely a considered choice, and won't take place overnight, it's certainly on the table for discussion.

So this is definitely a time when there can be major events within the family or your property that will set the stage for very different set of circumstances going forward, and this should be welcomed as a major new chapter.

Angels and Demons

The first solar eclipse of the year happens in the final degrees of Aries and it squares Pluto which is in your solar sixth house.

During this phase, which starts on the 20th of April, it's very important to detox. It's time to take your diet in hand and it may be important to eliminate a lot of substances from your diet. This is also a time when you have to be very careful of people in your life that are toxic.

In April and the following months, it's very important for you to think about your levels of self-control. You must reign yourself in, you must be focused and determined and it's also advisable for you to have time alone without distractions, so you can think clearly about what you want and need from situations you are looking to evoke.

The post April period, for about 3 months, is not just about eliminating bad food and detoxifying, it's also apart decluttering your life and getting rid of unwanted influences and activities that are not helping you attain what you need to in your life.

It's very important to think about your last year, the lessons you learnt and the things you began to release or move away from, this is another part of a process of being able to release resentment, anger and disappointment from your past and to move beyond those.

Doing some work with meditation and using affirmations or mantras to help you get into a positive mindset can be very useful. It's also important for you to mull over and analyze your dreams, keeping a dream journal can be a very helpful way to focus your attention on things coming up in dreams, that you may want to examine in day to day life.

This is also an excellent time for balancing your chakras, for seeing a spiritual or alternative healer that can work with your energies and remove blockages. You may also want to visit an acupressure, acupuncturist or chiropractor in order to complement the mental healing you are doing and improve your energy levels.

Energies and Essence - The right stuff.

The essence for January is taking care of business! It's important to be focused, direct and diligent, this is a time to get down to the nitty gritty, to organize the details and not to leave any stone unturned.

This is probably not the most creative month for Leo, it's more about understanding mechanisms, processes and requirements and making sure you understand these and get things right. Sometimes it's important to get to know the rules of the game before you are able to put your stamp on them, so this is a good month to make sure you understand exactly what's going to be required from any of your tasks, missions or career plans this year, and make sure you develop some excellent protocols.

This can also be a good time for setting up schedules, organizing the diary, taking note of important dates and basically just getting your head into gear, because sometimes once you have laid a structure it helps you to develop self-control, and the rest of the year can run that much smoothly, making sure less time is wasted and you can dedicate your precious time in the most effective way possible.

Affirmation: "I understand how important it is to respect my time and space, time is precious and I chose to use it wisely."

Love and Romance

With Jupiter, the ruler of your 5th solar house of romance, moving into Aries this energizes the field of romance and therefore social activities, dating and having date nights are really important.

You are likely to come across new romantic partners who are quite full on, who may be very assertive and who could want to boss you around literally sweeping you off your feet or dominating you in some cases. This can be exciting because you enjoy the great deal of warmth and enthusiasm they have, but in other cases you can find yourself a little bit overwhelmed. So there's two things going on here, relationships move quickly, they are very exciting and they have a great deal of emotional drama. On the other hand you can feel railroaded and you need to be careful of finding yourself in the clutches of a pushy partner who you don't really like but from whose influence you cannot escape.

In some cases you may love being flattered and bold-over, in other cases you need to say 'no' and say it quickly before you lose all power in a new relationship.

Career and Aspiration

During this month Leo have to be careful who you trust in the works sphere, you may come across someone who has a subversive agenda or who is not what they seem. It's very important for you to be careful in anything like recruitment or getting too friendly with new colleagues, because you may not understand fully what their intentions are, or what they have up their sleeve.

It pays to be a little bit cautious and suspicious and you should probably mind what you say, as not everyone is receptive to your ideas.

This is an excellent time for research, it's a good time for you getting more organized, streamlining processes and cutting out any dead wood. So as the year gets going, the best thing you can do is have a good clear out of your office, or in terms of your business get rid of any superfluous activities, associations and maybe let go of some staff who are not productive.

Changes at work can mean new routines and some extra skills

training. This is another month when you're a little preoccupied and could come over as cool.

Excitement and Motivation

This is a great month for you having fun with new friends and getting more involved in causes and activities that involve a lot of people. This may be an excellent month for going to concerts, attending sports events where you can feel the energy of the crowd and get really inspired, alternatively things like a protests and other political gatherings can be quite enjoyable for you.

Being more social and understanding your power and influence within the context of groups, can be good for your ego. In January, if you are alone, you may feel more powerless and isolated, however being out, getting into company and trying totally new things helps invigorate your sense of what is possible.

So it's great for you as the year kicks off to get off to the right start by being expansive, joining new organizations, perhaps becoming associated with a political group and then taking it from there, because one thing usually leads to another. Small steps tend to snowball, so all you really need to do is make the first move.

Marriage and Family

January is a time of quite intense emotions, you are more likely to react strongly to events, you are quite emotional and you feel instinctively compelled to do things. You're not a pushover, you're not easy to co-operate with and if your partner disagrees you can become very stubborn and intransigent.

Your protective instincts are aroused, and it's very hard to debate with you because you will exert your power and you will feel you're doing it for your partner's good, although that's not always the case. In some cases, though your instincts are good and you may be acting in your partner's best interests, your partner may not think so.

Whatever Leo are this month, you're not superficial, you cannot conceal your true feelings and your true intentions because these will erupt to the surface. So it's not a month where you can't be diplomatic, no matter how much you want to be, but this is actually quite powerful for relationships because it can lead to more honesty, and to a fundamental change that's quite necessary.

This is a month of evolution for Leo and that means inevitable evolution for the relationship, but for your partner it can sometimes feel like you are stirring up a hornet's nest or opening a Pandora's Box.

You're prone to self-doubt and vulnerable to your partner's criticism right now, you need support and encouragement. You may be too tense for good sex, you need to be encouraged to get outdoors, get fresh air and exercise. You may get turned on by a lovely back and shoulder rub. While you're not moody, you are edgy during this phase and likely to snap at you and be irritable, even though you are not up for a heated argument.

Money and Finance

This month it's wise for you to be cautious with money, you shouldn't do anything out of the ordinary or make any big moves. It's possibly a better month to leave things as they are, you don't have enough information yet to make decisions or to change anything radically.

The message in terms of money and finance is - if it ain't broke don't fix it and don't overthink it.

Living and Loving to the Full

This is actually an excellent month of the year to ignite romance, so whether you are in a new relationship or married, it's important for Leo to use your imagination, creativity and personality to start generating ideas for things to do together especially at the weekend.

In January, people are usually short of money because of the Christmas season, but it's important for you to think out the box, because there's still no reason that weekends have to be boring or mundane. This is not a month to focus on the chores or the housework, it's a month to live life to the full, to grab all the spare time available and use that for having little adventures with your partner.

So to get the romance going, it's time for you to be original and look for excitement again, not by doing anything too expensive, but just my going out of your way to do things that are more original and spontaneous.

Planetary Cautions

The Mercury retrograde period until the 19th affects your 6th solar house and you need to be careful of your health. While it may not be a good time to start a new diet, you may need to have a check-up and it's possible you will need to start learning about a new diet or way of eating to reduce weight or even tackle anxiety. It's important for you to understand any mineral or vitamin deficiencies you may have and to address these.

This is not a good time to merely go on a weight-loss diet, it's more of a time for lifestyle changes that can lead to permanent good health, rather than just fads which get boring and which you soon forget about. It may be a good idea to learn about a whole new way of eating, different routines around eating and also different psychological attitudes about eating can be very helpful.

It's time to address all the 'coping foods', now there are foods we all resort to in our busy lives because they help keep us going and get us over the line every day, these tend to be coffee, sugar, Coke and alcohol, but it's now time to start moving beyond those and seeing that with different ways of organizing your day, dealing with stress, dealing with your colleagues and other people, you can ditch those unhealthy coping foods, and develop other strategies to improve the way you deal with your daily routine.

This is also an excellent time to totally revolutionize your daily routines. Maybe you want to start working from home, job sharing, working different hours or finding new technology that can save you time. So a great way to spend time this month is investigating different computer programs or electronic equipment that could save you time or indeed do outsourcing.

Moon Magic

The new moon phase extends from the 21th of January to the 5th of February, this waxing phase is the perfect fortnight for new initiatives, setting plans, establishing goals, starting anything prospective and being proactive. This is the action phase, details below:

Mercury goes direct on 19th indicating that the communications sphere, short journeys, making contracts, financial dealings, investments, attending trade fairs, networking, large group activities and social media goals can gather stream and go ahead.

Sun Sextile Jupiter at the new moon favors new starts, new personal goals, health and diet changes and competitive activities. This is great for any role that requires confidence and making an impression on people.

Venus Conjunct Saturn indicates a good time to join a gym and think about changing your diet. This favors starting a new job, recruitment and medical matters.

This is not the best time for educational goals or new IT projects. Internet dating is not favored. This isn't a great time for PR, job interviews and dealing with authority.

Mars goes direct in Gemini on the 13th bringing about momentum for a life audit, pursuing hopes and dreams and any charitable goals. Group activities and networking are favored.

FEBRUARY

Essence and Energies - Come Together

This month balance and teamwork are very important.
Leo don't always find it easy to work in teams, particularly because
you are very individualistic, you are quite impatient and you have
your inimitable style, however the essence this month is being able to
grow closer to others by working with them and adjusting to some of
the their needs.

It's very important now to understand your strengths and weaknesses
and to be willing to work with people who have strengths in areas
where you don't so that you can form a team that compliments each
of you, but also so that you can learn from the other person. So it's
important to work with people you admire and respect, so that you
can watch and observe working closely with them, and therefore
develop more confidence in areas where you don't have much
experience.

So the key right now is thinking about what you don't have and what
you lack and looking for either advice, or preferably to work more
closely with people who are good at those things, because by
working with them in a respectful way, you can learn very quickly to
develop those skills, or enhance those areas where you feel weak or
lack confidence.

Affirmation: "I am open to learning from people who know more
than me and I am grateful for the benefit of their experience."

Love and Romance

This month new love affairs continue to move quickly, but there will also be obstacles in terms of the relationship as you may both be very busy and you may find that your schedules clash and so you guys are not able to spend as much time together as you would like. However this could actually add to the enthusiasm you both have for the relationship, absence makes the heart grow fonder.

The key in love this month is enjoyment and having fun together, and if you find that you're actually not having fun with a new partner, if you feel obligated or pressured, then you need to walk away very quickly. New relations right now should be filled with enjoyment, passion and a lot of excitement, and if they aren't or if they feel very stilted and laborious then they simply aren't meant to be.

If you recently come out of a relationship, this is an excellent time for healing, achieving closure and being philosophical about the events of the previous relationship. You should remember that in love, having philosophical understanding of the lessons learnt and the mistakes made is much more important than simply nursing a broken heart and looking for another partner to immediately to heal it.

Career and Aspiration

This is an excellent month in terms of your work for research and information gathering. Mercury is now direct but that doesn't mean that you should be full steam ahead in terms of making decisions, this is a time for being strategic, for planning and for looking at all the possible alternatives.

The key to success in your work right now is to dig deep, look further and seek to understand what others don't. So what you have to do, is go that extra mile in terms of gaining more data and thus getting better information, and that will put you ahead of your colleagues or the competition.

This is a very good month for Leo who happen to be in the medical field, you are more focused, your mind is incisive and this is an excellent time for you to contend with scientific and mathematical data.

Again, a certain amount of discretion and secrecy is very important this month, you need to be very careful with client boundaries and with respecting client confidentiality.

Adventure and Motivation

This is an excellent month for sporting activities and you can have a lot of fun being in the outdoors and enjoying adventure sports.

This is also a month where spiritual or religious activities done within the context of the church community can provide a lot of fun and satisfaction for Leo who have a religious calling.

Learning is part of the fun this month, so if you are at a loose end, doing things like going to museums, zoos and galleries can actually be a way of bringing a new dimension into your life, sparking an interest or piquing your curiosity.

During this time you may feel you have an edge over the competition, you may feel that you are winning, often there's a sense of slight ego and pride as you maybe see people who you usually compete with struggling, but you shouldn't let appearances deceive you, because they might be just taking a different route to yourself, which may be slower but more effective in the long run. So it's always important to watch and learn from what other people are doing rather than just assuming that what they are doing is wrong or ineffective.

Marriage and Family

This is one of the most important times of the year in terms of marriages and long-term relationships, this is when you may decide it's time to walk away from a bad relationship, and you should use this month to have difficult discussions with a partner about where the relationship is going.

In many cases, if the communication is diplomatic and objective, you can make a clean break from a bad relationship in order to move forward.

In terms of marriage in general, it's time to stop beating about the bush. This is a month for you and your partner to be honest about the challenges you face in terms of your relating to each other, and also in terms of struggles you face as a couple. This is not a time for escapism or delusion, this is the time for you and your partner to take a cold light of day appraisal of the realities of the situation, and resolve to work through them in a systematic way.

This is an excellent time for planning things with a partner in terms of what the goals and objectives of your year should be and how best to cope with any difficulties you guys see coming.

Money and Finance

While last month, in terms of money, it was a nothing-burger, this month you are more fortunate in terms of finances. If you have been having any problem with gaining credit or taking on a loan, this may be a good month to find a suitable loan at a good rate.

If you receive a lot of your income via donations, subscriptions or tips, this can be an excellent month. If you do any vlogging or affiliate marketing, this is an excellent time to push the boat out and to be a lot more proactive about getting new subscribers or encouraging people to your website to increase donations and subscriptions.

A family member may be willing to lend some money to you or you may benefit by the fact that your marriage partner gets a rise.

Living and Loving to the Full

This month it's very important for Leo to work at foreplay and affection. Tenderness and romance are a key to unlocking the secrets of your love life. You certainly need to be observant and patient in terms of trying to understand your partner's intimate preferences, and therefore suggesting exotic little experiments or activities that you might undertake together is ideal.

Beyond the romance, physical touch is very important but this doesn't have to be sexualized. Touch can be very healing, so even for Leo who haven't been having a lot of intimacy with their partner, the best way to begin again is just by increasing the level of touch, and that could be a friendly foot rub, a little shoulder rub, an arm round the shoulders while you watch TV etc. It doesn't have to be full on and very overt, it's just important to reintroduce touch throughout the day as a way of showing not only affection, but also tenderness, care and compassion. You should remember that a small touch often says a lot more than just words, for example saying, "Are you alright?" through a gentle hand on the shoulder.

Planetary Cautions

This is a month when it's probably best for you to avoid getting any dental work, getting a tattoo or making any radical changes to your appearance.

It's important for you to take care of your bone health, you should take on board extra calcium and be extra careful of your diet. This is a time of year when can feel very drained, depleted and you are far more vulnerable to infection and illness therefore it's important for you to have a balanced diet, reduce all alcohol and improve leafy green vegetable intake and fresh food.

So what you have to avoid this month, is risks with your health and you should think health first and everything else second.

Moon Magic

The new moon phase extends from the 20th of February to the 7th of March, this waxing phase is the perfect fortnight for new initiatives, setting plans, establishing goals, starting anything prospective and being proactive. This is the action phase, details below:

The waxing phase is excellent for business management, career planning, job interviews, corporate events and PR. Dealing with authority is successful.

Not a good time for marriage and engagement. New business associations are not favored. Not a great time to reboot a relationship or try marriage counseling.

Property matters and home improvements are not favored.

MARCH

Energies and Essence - **"The echoes that you find, in the windmills of your mind."**

This month escapism and using your imagination is vital. It's important to know that you don't have all the answers and you don't have to, often it's invigorating and emotionally stimulating to feel in the dark and to take a path that you are unsure of, for there could be valuable lessons to learn and things to uncover.

What is essential is invisible to the eye, only the heart can see rightly, so be guided by your gut and your institution.

Clarity and understanding comes not from logic, bit from a place deep within. Often escaping via art, movies or music can help you connect with something that was lost or missing in your life.

Affirmations and creative visualization can be very useful for escapism but also for reprogramming your psychology in a more positive way.

Affirmation: "I trust in my innate optimism and creativity to help me find solutions to all problems."

Love and Romance

With Venus and Jupiter conjunct in Aries, this is one of the best months of the year for love, this can be an excellent time for you to join dating clubs, go to social events and look for love, because it's a high possibility that Cupid will strike. If you're already in a relationship, things should really be feeling great now and you should be developing a rapport and should feel warm and comfortable, yet still excited in the relationship.

This is an excellent time for relationships that are fairly new, after a long period of you being single, these will have a particular amount of excitement and enchantment.

The great thing about romance for Leo now is that romance is extremely inspiring, rejuvenating and it can help replenish your soul.

New relationships can have an extremely healing and also a calming influence, so it's not just about dating for the sake of attraction or companionship or sex, there's often a spiritual dimension right now to relationships, which again has a healing quality.

Career and Goals

You need a fair degree of autonomy in your work this March. Now that you're done all your research, you feel like it's time to forge ahead and it could be resentful of others becoming involved in your work.

A key aspect of career development now is independence, you no longer want to be dependent on others for support and encouragement. The best thing you can do is reach within for ideas and insight rather than look externally for someone to lead you.

This is the time where you have confidence simply because you don't have a lot of doubt about what you're doing, you tend to be aware that the timing is now right, that you need to act and that. Fortune favors the brave.

Adventure and Motivation

This is quite a lucky time for Leo, it's great for you to get involved in competitive activities, particularly sporting, as these can be both successful and very rewarding.

Another avenue where you can have a lot of fun is by taking leadership in community projects. If there's any issue affecting your community or your social group, this is a time when you should become a spearhead, a spokesperson or leader with new ideas on how to problem solve.

This is a particularly rewarding time for Leo's who work in careers where they give advice and guidance, because you can have a lot of fun working with people and helping to empower them as well as helping them along the lines of their own personal growth.

Work with groups of people is rewarding and fun for you right now.

Illusions can be comforting but they can also be regressive and so hidden truth must be discovered or rediscovered, so what you are seeing now can be seen for what it is. So search for the hidden forces or illusions within your own life that actually magnify fear, even it feels safe in the short run.

This is the time the strengthen your boundaries and ensure that you are doing as much for yourself and your own development as you are giving in terms of your energy to others. Refocus energy inwards and even if you cannot do anything concrete, make sure you establish some new goals which ensure that you have a route out of any situation which has entrapped you.

Marriage and Family

This month marriage is in need of an injection of romance and compassion. It is important for you to show understanding to your partner and awareness of their needs, and if you feel that your partner has been little bit neglectful of your needs, it's definitely time for you to say so, and make sure that there is an understanding that goes both ways.

This may not be the best month for you and your partner to make decisions, you guys are both rather emotional this month that's why things like romance, escapism and renewing the emotional bond are very important. However, decisions of a more pragmatic nature that require a sanguine, cool-headed approach should be delayed for now. So I'm giving you guys the green light for romance, renewed understanding, developing more compassion and improving intimacy, but I'm thinking that you should delay more important financial, property or family decisions until another month.

Money and Finance

This month can be excellent for you obtaining money from family members, from donations, subscriptions and royalties once again.

You should refrain from taking on any more debt this month and you should avoid any major decisions because you don't have as much information as you need.

Most financial matters are not as straightforward as you thinks, and it's very important for you to understand the fine print and the legal detail in terms of any loans you are currently taking on, any tax changes or in the claiming of benefits or insurance.

You also need to be aware of changes in tax laws or social security laws, so that you can either adjust your finances or take advantage of opportunities.

Living and Loving to the Full

This month, the way Leo can Living and Loving to the Full is by letting go, and that means you have to into romantic situations with a clear head. In terms of intimate situations, you need to master how to leave all your worries at the door. So sometimes a little bit of meditation or mindfulness just to get yourself in the mood, to release of anxieties and to place all your stresses in a different space outside your bubble, can actually help you to enjoy intimacy with your partner and to get so much more from it.

Partners know when their mate's mind is elsewhere, so what you need to do is to have your mind fully engaged in the passion and the tenderness of the moment, and your partner will observe that intuitively, they'll pick up those signs and will know they have your attention, and that way the moment is so much more sweet.

To help with this letting go and escapism, is to take all the phones and the devices and leave them outside the bedroom, and preferably the remote control for the television as well, otherwise these serve as distractions when you should be focusing on love.

Planetary Cautions

You should avoid any extreme diets or fasting this month. It's best to use gentle techniques to lose weight and improve health. Sudden extreme exercises or endurance sports are also not favored.

This is not a good time for recruitment or delegating and outsourcing as the quality can be disappointing.

It's important for you to work with unions and your staff rather than against.

If you're employed you should steer clear of intrigue, office gossip and anything questionable.

This is not to best month for highly analytical work, it's far better for lateral, right brain thinking and creativity.

Moon Magic

The new moon phase extends from the 21st of March to the 6th of April, this waxing phase is the perfect fortnight for new initiatives, setting plans, establishing goals, starting anything prospective and being proactive. This is the action phase, details below:

The waxing phase is excellent for education and communication goals. This is a great time for research and multitasking.

This favors goals related to improving relationships with coworkers, recruiting and outsourcing. Health matters are favored and new diets and health kicks are successful.

Career moves and new business ventures are not favored in the waxing phase. Not a great time for PR or job interviews. Public speaking is not favored.

Short distance travel, cyber dating or joining dating apps is not successful.

Not a great time for seeking a loan or taking on debt. This is not favorable for new sexual relationships or prep agreements. Tax and accounting or financial management matters are not favored. Not a good time to manage other people's money.

Energies and Essence - "The long and winding road."

One of the key characteristics of Leo is your optimistic, sunny and buoyant approach and the essence to connect with this month is your innate positivity.

We all have our ups and downs in life, and things aren't always perfect, but one thing for sure is that your natural state of mind and state of heart is to be buoyant and optimistic, it always helps to look at the positives because there's always light at the end of the tunnel and always something to be learnt from your experiences.

So the essence this month is for you to look for the positive in every situation, and to lead through your positivity. So it's not just a case of feeling rather resilient and buoyant inside, it's about cultivating and working on your positivity levels and then radiating it out to other people to help inspire and support them.

Even if you feel a little bit blue, it's very important now to put on a brave face and to show others an optimistic attitude, because when you inspire others it lifts everyone and it will in turn lift you.

Affirmation: "I am filled with divine energy that imbues me with lightness and positive energy."

Love and Romance

This month Leo has to be persevering in love, you are on the right track and things are beginning to develop nicely, so even if you feel that you're not quite hitting the right notes with a new person, you should continue to persevere. You're in high spirits and you are presenting yourself well, so the opportunities are still ripe for exciting new developments in romance, so you should hang tight and watch this space.

Romance seems to be one of the most important things going on in your life right now, and it can be quite a distraction. So the key is this: if you have to be strongly focused on your career and you already have enough on your plate, maybe it's better for you to veer away from the dating scene, but if there's an empty space in your life and you have time on your hands, then extra social activities, dating apps, dating nights and single nights all get the green light.

You'll probably be evasive if your partner is asking a lot of questions about your plans or if your partner is attempting to make long term plans for you guys as a couple. You're going to be Luke warn about any long term plan set in stone, however you're certainly happy to throw ideas about and brainstorm. Use this as an opportunity for discussion about your options and throw around some ideas, especially brand new ideas that offer exciting options.

Career and Aspirations

With Mars in Cancer, this is not the best time for you to enter extremely competitive, demanding, physically challenging activities. This is also not a good time for you to challenge the establishment. You should use this time for research, perfection and for thoroughly understanding what you may be up against.

You could call this a month of pit-stops where you have to recharge your batteries, get mentally into the right frame of mind and prepare for attack and action when it comes to June.

You need advice and you seek reassurance from older family members especially men. You may choose to spend more time with your dad or even at work, if you have a senior colleague whom you trust.

Adventure and Motivation

This month it's important for Leo to recognize both your inner and outer strength and how these work together in helping you to be strong, assertive and positive when opening new opportunities for yourself.

This month you must remember while embarking on your new adventures that it's not just a material thing, it's about how to make you feel the value your efforts creates for you and others.

You're likely to have a high energy level this month which is perfect for vigorous activities, be they sporting activities, singing, entertaining or anything which requires a lot of gusto. You certainly have that oomph and you can create a positive aura for other people too. This month the room definitely lights up when you walk in, and even if the people you know are having a tough time, you are certainly a beacon of love and positivity.

Marriage and Family

This month Leo may find yourself on the horns of a moral dilemma in terms of love relationships. There's almost a crossroads where you must choose between doing the thing that you instinctively knows is right, or taking the low road. Often taking the low road is easier because it is conflict avoiding and simplified, whereas going with your integrity means an element of risk i.e. risk involving conflict, disruption to the direction of your life or even interruption in terms of your relationship harmony.

During this month Leo value system is often challenged, it may even be that your partner is doing something that you strongly disagree with and feel that is wrong, however because it's something that your partner is passionate about, it's going to be difficult raising that issue.

However the choice is his, if you don't choose wisely now you may encounter this problem in a different form in a few months' time when it will be even trickier to deal with.

Money and Finance

During this month Leo should avoid spending any more money investing in your business or business expansion. You should also avoid spending any money on education to further your career, or on corporate entertaining or public relations.

However after Mercury goes direct in Taurus next month these activities can resume.

This may also not be a good month for you to invest in assets, for example gold, silver, antiques or art as you cannot be sure of the real value.

If you do invest this month or spend your money on a considered purchase, you should make sure you keep the receipt, guarantees, warranties or some sort of 30 day money back guarantee.

Living and Loving to the Full

Enhancing love magic this month is about taking a long-term vision about what can be achieved, so even if things are rocky or not perfect at the moment, there's all the time in the world to work on the relationship and to improve things, and so there's no cause whatever to feel despondent. Even if you're trying things romantically or sexually that aren't hitting the right notes right now, that's no excuse to stop trying because soon things will click

There's added value in love relationships this month when Leo acknowledges that you and your partner are sharing a journey together. The months or years which you have been together represents something unique in time that you guys share, something that will always bind you together and you have created memories will last a lifetime. There's often a philosophical sense of purpose in understanding the role that you are both playing in each other's personal evolution and that can make the relationship seem more precious.

This month is definitely a test of the respect you have and the trust you have for each other, and if you do push the boundaries of the relationship and try and push the relationship in a direction that it hasn't gone in before, you may be quite surprised at some of the outcomes. You may see sides to your partner that are a little bit disconcerting, and which startle you. This may be the month when you realize that there are some things about your partner you never knew, or never properly understood, or maybe your partner is developing in a way that is a little bit surprising. So this creates some challenges to the relationship, but remember all relationships are dynamic, they don't stay the same and that's why you need to be open minded and adaptable in relationships so that you can grow together rather than holding each other back.

Planetary Cautions

With Mercury retrograde in Taurus conjunct Uranus the worst thing you can do now is jump from the frying pan into the fire. Right now there's a huge amount of impetuousness and impetus to act, however while it might feel that you're being pushed into a decision, you're actually got more time then you think and you should use this time wisely.

It's highly likely that you are under a lot of pressure right now, but things could do a 180 turn in a month's time, so decisions that look good now may look very different in a month's time. Thus you need to buy yourself time and delay because things could look very different next month.

Mercury goes retrograde on the 21st in your tenth house and so this is a period when there are changes and indecision in your career. This is not a good time for you to make a major career move. It's a time when you should amass information, investigate, keep your nose to the ground and be flexible and alert to potential opportunities or problems which you need to circumvent. In this period you have a lot of conflicting ideas about your future and you cannot commit or make decisions. This is not a good time to get married or engaged as you will be in two minds and this could mean the relationship gets off on a shaky footing.

Moon Magic

The new moon phase extends from the 20th of April to the 5th of March, this waxing phase is the perfect fortnight for new initiatives, setting plans, establishing goals, starting anything prospective and being proactive. This is the action phase, details below:

The waxing phase is excellent for making changes to your routines to improve health and tackle bad habits. A good period for psychological understanding, tackling fears and being more self-aware. New relationships are passionate but possessiveness can be an issue.

Mercury retrograde in Taurus on the 21st in Taurus indicates the need for caution in all public speaking or social media posts. It's a time for due diligence and careful preparation. New career, business and management strategies may not go as planned, careful research and back up plans are needed. Not a good time for a totally new career or job interviews.

Energies and Essence - "Had the guts got the glory!"

This month is one where you require resolution and closure before Mars enters Leo in the third week when it's all hands on deck as you feel a powerful surge in energy and want to get cracking on.

If things have not gone as you have planned or are not going very well, you must examine yourself and ask if there are inner doubts which are bringing about this outer frustration. Do not be scared to ask yourself some fundamental questions about life, your past and your relationship to the past. How much is the past part of the present and is it over represented? Which of your values impact your life most right now and are you getting your priorities right. Getting to the heart of what you believe and how those beliefs govern your lifestyle is key to resolving the nagging questions and anxieties which plague you.

So a certain amount of emotional spring cleaning is vital so that you can make the most of the Mars energy for leadership and innovation in your life as it kicks in later this month.

Affirmation: "I am not a victim of my past, my fears or my doubts, my light is bigger than all the emotions that cast a shadow."

Love and Romance

With Jupiter in Taurus, this is a really important time for you to build in terms of love relationships. Now is the time to be pragmatic and to talk about the relationship's future, and definitely to get closer intimately.

You can feel very romantic and passionate and right now your desire levels are quite high so it's important for you guys to spoil each other and revel in each other's company. So the more you and your partner show each other generosity and warmth, the better for the relationship.

It's important to remember that this year relationships can easily become possessive, and that will be in evidence this month. So Leo and your partner need to be alert to possessiveness creeping in, and you guys need to be mindful of the fact that you both do want to own each other simply because of the strength of feeling, but this must not degenerate into something very negative or controlling.

Career and Aspiration

This month Jupiter enter Taurus which is wonderful news for the career, aims and aspirations of Leo. Any plans and ideas or brainstorming that you have done so far in the year, now start to take shape and take form, meaning you can get really excited and stuck in.

With Mercury going direct in Taurus on the 21st, you can again go ahead with plans, make contracts or pay for educational courses that will help you to achieve the necessary knowledge for the next step in your career.

This is a very important month in terms of you communicating with your clients and customers, you need to make sure that information is timely, concise and useful. It's also very important for you to update your website in order to increase the relevance of information and the ease with which your customers can contact you. It may also be important for you to have backup communication systems and software, so everything should be saved on a hard copy as should all your client lists and databases.

Adventure and Motivation

Mars goes into Leo in the middle of the month and that means it's an excellent time for you to be proactive and assertive. It's time for you to look after number one and you can get a lot of satisfaction and fun through contact sports and athletic activity.

This is a great time for you to join the gym and kick-start physical fitness regimes.

This can be a very exciting time for Leo to adopt more technology in your business, as being innovative and an early adopter can help set you apart from the competition and it can also create a great deal of excitement for you.

A fancy new phone or labor saving device could also be something that gets your motor running, so you may enjoy shopping around the technical stores for interesting, hot off the press devices.

Marriage and Family

This month your marriage faces challenges arising from the outside world, and these could stem from changes in political and social terms. There are important decisions for you and your partner to make together, this is a month where team playing and cooperation is very important.

It's likely that Leo and your partner will interpret and react to different situations in the outside world in different ways, because your emotional reactions or understanding of these events may differ. This causes temporary conflict or bickering.

What you both have to do is focus on the facts and the strategies of how to deal with the situations, rather than focusing on how you both feel about situations emotionally. It's time to take logical and systematic steps to ensure the security of your family, particularly financially and in terms of where you are living.

Sometimes events in the outside world tend to focus Leo and your partner on the strengths you have in terms of the relationship, and working together. So while events could drive some couples apart, in many cases they will drive you guys back together as you form a united front.

Money and Finance

This month is a good month for budgeting and being more organized in terms of your finances, it is a good time to tackle admin and also improve your accounting or record keeping methods.

Money can be well spent paying for advice, alternatively paying for an accountant or tax advisor who can help you get your affairs in order or get a clear of grasp of what is going on - especially as there are likely to be changes in tax laws very soon.

This is a good month to make investments but these should be risk-free, so any investments you makes into your own business or in terms of your pension are sensible, but you shouldn't speculate or play the stock market.

Living and Loving to the Full

With Venus in Cancer this month, the way to ignite love magic is through escapism and romance. So this is the ideal time to book a romantic getaway, and if you guys like the idea of a log cabin or even a city escape for just the pair of you, that would be an excellent idea.

It's ideal if you can leave the children with Grandma or a babysitter, just so that you can have some private time and that private time should be spent enjoying each other's company rather than feeling the need to rush about, meet people or sightsee.

It's almost like you guys need a mini romantic retreat to recharge your love batteries and to make sure that you get into a space where you are relaxed enough to speak about the things that are closest to your heart, without feeling stressed rushed, or like your relationship is last on the list.

Planetary Cautions

This month Leo should definitely avoid DIY, home improvements or undertaking anything strenuous work involving changes to your home or garden.

You should be especially careful if you're using any saws, drills or electrical equipment in the home environment, in fact you should really avoid doing that and rather get a professional in.

This is not a good time to have family over to stay, because there can be unpleasant arguments and eruptions, as it's generally quite an emotional time and being around family too much could mean salt being rubbed in wounds and creating uncomfortable situations.

Moon Magic

The new moon phase extends from the 19th of May to the 3rd of June this waxing phase is the perfect fortnight for new initiatives, setting plans, establishing goals, starting anything prospective and being proactive. This is the action phase, details below:

The waxing phase is excellent for marriage, engagement and dare nights. It's great for reviving love.

It's also good for business and creative collaboration.

You should be cautious with strenuous exercise and competitive contact sports. You must address repressed anger. This is not a good time for holistic medicine or alternative medicine.

New romance, dating a singles nights are not favored. A brand new business involving children's toys, sports or entertaining is not favored. Not a great time for launching a creative product.

Health and dietary changes are successful. Moderate exercise routines are important. A good time for service related business, recruitment or skills training. Working with animals is favored.

Energies and Essence – Take the initiative.

This month is about being decisive and taking action. Get busy, no excuses, make your mark.

This is a phase of action, with Mars in Leo and Jupiter in Taurus, you must make your mark on the world, be competitive, expressive and creative.

If there's anything you desire it's time to go for it. It's ok to be ambitious and to put yourself first. You should asset your claim, it's your life and no one can live it for you. Take responsibility for your future and own it.

Take the risk of possible upsetting others by being honest and living your life your way, as they will respect you more in the long run

Affirmation: "I value my destiny and I seize the chances that come my way fearlessly"

Love and Romance

Leo needs to understand the difference between sympathy and love this month. Friends with benefits situations are toxic as this encourages need and expectations in one party leading to hurt and disappointment.

In ongoing love relationships, Leo enjoys making your home welcoming for your new partner or friends in general. You'll find new relationships enjoy a more stable, fruitful and relaxing time and you guys can certainly afford to indulge a little and treat yourselves.

Single Leo is in a wonderful position to find a partner that truly brings a special spark into your life. You'll have high standards however, and will aim for someone who has the same level of dedication, enthusiasm and loyalty as you do.

Leo feel compelled to be more assertive in relationships and your stubborn, uncompromising side comes out and yet this can play in your favor as your partner is quite reassured when you are decisive and set out a clear agenda. No relationship benefits from vacillation or woolly thinking as it seeds confusion and even distrust, however Leo have an inner resolve this month which leads to clear communication and progress in terms of relationship issues.

Career and Motivation

Sudden changes in the wider economy or your management structure could mean you have to take initiative and make do. This month you have to wing it, it's a time when nothing goes to plan and technology can break down. Often others throw in the towel, so you have to show your mettle for crisis leadership.

This can be a stressful month, it's unpredictable and turbulent but as long as you keep your head about you can make a valuable impression on your professional peers.

Your positive mood will affect other people you meet and this is the perfect time to attend a social gathering or corporate event. You may attract money or meet people that offer you some financial benefit.

You also have a great ability to express your creativity, with a special talent for creating harmony in sound, texture or form.

Adventure and Motivation

While you need exercise and fresh air to release the huge amount of discordant energy within you, you must especially careful when operating machinery, doing adventure sports, using power tools, or driving motor vehicles, as sudden and unexpected events are likely because of the explosive energies generated by Mars in Leo square Uranus.

While exercise can be beneficial, your mind must be totally focused on what you're doing or else an injury can occur.

Time by yourself doing something completely novel and intellectually interesting can be the best remedy this month. You may get a lot of satisfaction by gaming.

You can have a lot of fun with strangers at an event involving exchanging ideas and learning.

Marriage and Family

This isn't a great month for important or contentious discussions in the family context, you're
more likely to fly off the handle, over-reacting to simple remarks and releasing pent up frustration in unhelpful ways.

You can be stubborn and pig headed - "my way or the highway".

You're not very thoughtful and yet you will regret harsh words said in the heat of the moment. You're quite stressed which manifests as impatience, recklessness and impulsiveness in your actions.

In marriage, you could have misplaced priorities, which may eventually be compromising to the future. You may find that you're more avoidant and distracted and unable to focus on the problems or long-term goals in your marriage. You could also be busy working on ideas or plans without taking time to consult your partner.

You must now ready to become accountable and responsible for the direction of your marriage, you must pursue your independence, but also encourage your loved ones to be strong enough to make their own decisions.

Money and Finance

This is a month of good karma and reward.

Abundance, success, and material security increases as does your executive confidence in terms of making important financial decisions. You may find that after a period of hard work, you suddenly have all the tools, tricks and cash you need to feel good about the future of your business or your security.

Responsibility in the past now pays off and you have a small excess meaning you can balance enjoying life's pleasures, with practicality in terms of savings and business development.

You're adept at finding good deals, and making savings without having to compromise on quality.

Living and Loving to the Full

What you need to do to get the most from this month is to understand what you most need your partner to do or change, and what you yourself most need to do for yourself to change in terms of the relationship, and then you guys need to talk about this openly. The great thing this month is that you and your partner are more secure and thus more receptive to hear criticism, although this need not be harsh, and suggestions for a way forward.

So, time to get your own ducks in a row and have constructive but relaxed conversions and feel the rays of sunlight shine into your love life.

Planetary Cautions

You should avoid business ventures with friends or professional peers as they may be on a wild goose chase. This month it's easy to get swept away by hype and marketing waffle, so it's really important for you to understand the true nature of any financial or business opportunity.

You should very careful of Ponzi schemes and social media driven projects as these could be white elephants.

You should avoid traveling with friends, and in general new networking activities. This is not a great month for implementing large scale technological projects.

You should avoid protects, crowds and political events.

Moon Magic

The new moon phase extends from the 18th of June to the 3rd of July this waxing phase is the perfect fortnight for new initiatives, setting plans, establishing goals, starting anything prospective and being proactive. This is the action phase, details below:

The waxing phase is tricky for extreme sports or image changes. It's also not wonderful for totally new activities or ventures. Spiritual advice should be taken with caution.

Networking, making new friends and group activities are successful. New financial activities and investments are favored, it's a good time for major purchases i.e. a car or assets for your business.

It's a good time for publishing, higher education and advertising to increase your profile. Long haul travel is successful. This is not ideal for internet dating, short trips or social media marketing and IT projects.

New career directions are favored.

Marriage and engagement are not favored. New romance and dating during the waxing phase is not successful.

Energies and Essence – "I chose to travel each and every highway."

The essence this month is connecting with your core and finding an inner safe place, a place of retreat and a place of calm.

Whatever is happening in the world, in your relationships etc. it's important right now not to look outside for answers. You have to connect with your inner wisdom and understand that within you is the Divine knowledge to guide you through any situation, and what you really have to do is to shut out the noise the hubbub or the distractions so that you can listen to that voice.

Just imagine you are trying to listen to a very beautiful, romantic piece of music, and your neighbors are blaring heavy metal - that's what it's like every day when your inner voice tries to send us messages via coincidences and little signs, but it's struggling to be heard because we are always bombarding ourselves with activities or people who are very demanding of us.

That's why it's important to find a place in your life where you can be calm, secluded and possibly do some meditation or techniques that bring you a sense of solace, and where you can listen to your intuition and ESP.

Affirmation: "I resolve to connect with the call of my higher self and follow my divine purpose."

Love and Romance

During this month you're often caught up in the moment, there is the potential for sudden romantic and sexual experiences. You tend to get caught up in the beauty or excitement of the moment, which can draw you into the pursuit of shallow pleasures, which while they may allure you, and bring excitement, there may be little else to them.

Recently developed love relationships may suffer sudden separations, which may arise because Leo suddenly see things for how they really are, or perhaps you both need a step back to allow the dust to settle and to redraw the boundaries.

Volatility will mark any romantic liaisons and their ability to last depends on your guys' capacity to understand and tolerate each other's passions and quirks.

It's really important for you to understand the 'shop window effect', most people don't share their problems particularly on Facebook and they only put up pictures and posts about the great things in their life. I call this the 'shop window effect' when you are selling something in your shop, you are only going to put your most fashionable, glamorous and exciting things in the window, any seconds or damaged items you will hide away in the stockroom, and people do that on social media. So it's very important not to compare yourself to others_ curated 'shop window' as this leads to disappointment and unnecessary despair.

Career and Aspiration

Unreliability in your business relationships and contacts can create stress, especially if you are depending on people to keep their word. You have to be able to rely on yourself and you have to have a plan B that you can use to fall back on.

You may suddenly decide that you really need to do something different with your business, and you may seek greater freedom from red tape or authority figures or regulations that are limiting your expansion possibilities.

This July is about disrupting your accustomed patterns of relating to both authority or established norms in your business. New relationships or new mentors can emerge which open your mind to different alternatives.

Disruptions during this period and challenges in maintaining the usual smooth relationships and connections are a cue for you to understand the limitations of these established relationships, and how different ones are needed.

Adventure and Motivation

This month research and problem solving is very exciting to you. You enjoy looking for answers, toying with technology and being inventive.

You may get a kick out of playing with engines, working with music processing equipment, film editing or doing anything else which requires fine tuning to create a perfect end product.

You're quite perfectionistic and you enjoy working through issues and untangling them.

This is an excellent time for you to probe below the surface to ferret out secrets and find unique solutions and answers.

Marriage and Family

No matter how much you seek harmony, conflict is inevitable this month because karmic and psychic energies are very disruptive.

Anything you had suppressed in terms of anger, hostility, resentment tends to leak out even when you're doing your best to be calm and reasonable.

It's very important for you to control your thoughts as negative thoughts are intuitively picked up by your partner and they may act them out.

So this month it's not what you say, it's about what you don't.

In addition, any secrets you're been keeping or indiscretions can suddenly be revealed against your will.

In marriage, this is an excellent time for debate and discussion, and if you feel that you need to apologize over something it's really good to do it now, because your apology will be appreciated and accepted. It can be a time where you often feel unappreciated in relationships, so it's important to be able say to your partner, "Hey, where is mine, I have needs and my needs need to be met!" So it's quite ok to be demanding in relationships, because there must be fairness and balance or you can feel quite resentful.

Money and Finance

It's important for Leo to fully commit to assignments and ensure that you get over the finish line efficiently.

This is an excellent time for deadlines and also for showing absolutely loyalty to your long term clients and customers. You must do the best you can, no short cuts and no excuses.

Money comes your way when you are clear on your sense of duty and when you understand your strengths and play to that.

This is also a time when good routines and sticking with your tried and trusted methods lead to accomplishments.

Living and Loving to the Full

If your love life is feeling rather stale and unsatisfactory, it could be because you're not being honest about what you want or maybe you're not making enough effort to take emotional risks or speak your truth.

Even successful relationships are desperate for change and you guys may feel a bit restless, which could lead to arguments, especially about how much time you spend at work respectively. It's time to prioritize the relationship. Make sure that you guys carve out time in your hectic lives to just be with one another, or do something spontaneous to bring a much needed breath of fresh air into your relationship.

Planetary Cautions

Differences of opinion with colleagues are likely, which can lead to more significant disagreements if you dig your heels in, which you may have to do on a matter of principle.

Although you have very strong ideas that you feel intuitively you must promote, the more you push these attitudes however, the more likely you are to encounter opposition to them, which will become quite intense. You must be diplomatic and cautious when expressing your ideas as you could be setting a lot of backstabbing and opposition in motion just by doing what you think is right.

This is a period of cat and mouse, and it's a mental challenge working with others and being true to yourself without running into a minefield of agendas.

Moon Magic

The new moon phase extends from the 17th of July to the 30th of July, this waxing phase is the perfect fortnight for new initiatives, setting plans, establishing goals, starting anything prospective and being proactive. This is the action phase, details below:

The waxing phase is not a great time for competitive activities, events requiring physical stamina and brand new experiences. It's not a good time to do something you're a complete novice at.

Not a good time for medical matters, new diets or joining a gym. Recruitment and outsourcing aren't favored. Not a good time for a new pet.

An excellent time for new investment, financial planning and analysis. A good time to make major purchases for your business. Good for stability in relationships.

AUGUST

Energies and Essence – "I got a new sensation
In perfect moments
That's impossible to refuse"

*This month is a wonderful opportunity to do something you have
never done before, it's time to be a little bit radical, a little bit
controversial. You may want to change your image, get a snazzy new
haircut, a new wardrobe or simply make a statement to the world
that you are going to launch a brand new you.*

*This is an ideal month to make changes within your career, or you
can change your whole game plan when it comes to how you want to
approach your life. It's never too late for a brand new attitude, this
is certainly a time to be positive, so whatever is going on in your life,
whether you feel happy, stuck or you feel a little bit lost or blue, this
is the time to strike out, grab the bull by the horns and make a stand.*

*You should give a strong message to yourself and those around you
that change will be happening and it will be for the better. Use
affirmations to confirm your intention, and then take positive
concrete steps to effect the change in practical ways, and remember
you don't have to make big steps, sometimes only doing a small thing
slightly differently opens a door that leads to a huge rush of air. Just
think that even in a warm room, a small crack can create a big
draught, so just a small glimmer of something new can create a
massive draught of change in your life.*

*Affirmation: "I have a right to live my life authentically and to renew
myself periodically!"*

Love and Romance

This can be an exciting month for relationships, but can also be a time when things tend to fall apart. Leo is impatient and your pushy side comes to the fore, so relationships with water signs or more sensitive signs can suffer, whereas relationships with other fire signs or earth signs can become more dynamic.

Because you're got a high level of energy, you and your partner need to be getting out and doing activities like dancing, attending sports events where there's a lot of self-expression and cheering etc. as you can really let off steam together.

This is definitely not a good month for visiting your parents or attending family events where you have to stand on ceremony, be very well behaved and conformist. This is an excellent month for doing things totally out of the box and just having a period of being like teenagers and free spirits again.

Career and Aspiration

This month is a difficult one when it comes to teamwork and working with others in any capacity, Leo is ideally placed where you work off your own bat and to your own initiative. It's very important for you to see results from what you does or you can feel very demoralized.

The more you have control over what you are doing and how you are doing it, the more you will feel inspired by what you do. However, if you feel that you don't have a lot of control, that you are not appreciated or that your input is not acknowledged, you can become lazy and avoidant and may look for ways to dither or distract yourself from what should be done.

If you are suffering a lack of inspiration in your work, this is an ideal time to take a holiday, get away from it all and recharge your creative batteries. It may be the case that you are just totally depleted and need to take a step away in order to indulge in some thorough R&R.

Adventure and Motivation

With sun in Leo this month, squaring both Jupiter and Uranus, this is definitely a time for you to seek adventure and excitement in your spare time.

You have a strong need to get the adrenaline going and this is another great month for outdoor activity and exciting new sports or creative pursuits.

This is the best time of year for you to step out and begin a totally new activity where you feel a lot of instant gratification and personal fulfilment.

It's time for you to seek novelty and you may need to upset a few people or ruffle a few feathers, and this should not deter you as this is all about you, your individualism and your levels of fulfilment in life.

Marriage and Family

With Venus going in retrograde in Leo last month and being retrograde in Leo for the whole of this month, this is an important time for Leo and your partner to examine their priorities and values.

It's easy for couples to focus on disagreements in terms of the superficial value of those disagreements, but often underlying these is a lack of understanding of where each other is currently at in terms of their top priorities and needs.

When couples first get together they spend a lot of time getting to know each other, and it's an important feature of dating. However once people get married they stop learning about each other and this is a problem because people change and they evolve, so occasionally in marriage it's important to relearn about each other and that is exactly what Leo needs to do this month.

You can be quite unpredictable and you tend to find the things which usually satisfy you or comfort you no longer do. It's a time when you're willing to try quite radical new options, your partner may feel you are acting out of character. Your demands of your partner can be different to your usual needs, your partner may find it hard to know what you want and thus you have to be a little patient and also tolerant.

Money and Finance

This is a great time for hustling, it's a good time for you to multitask and for you to use your creativity to open new avenues for making money.

This is a good time for you to become more self-reliant and independent and it definitely favors those Leo who are moving to working for themselves or who work on commission. Energy and drive leads to profits, so the more you can influence your own income by working harder, engaging more with clients or being proactive the better.

Leo on fixed salaries can feel quite frustrated this month, but there's no reason you can't use your spare time to develop an extra activity that can generate a stream of income.

This is not a good time to apply for a loan and to rely on passive income, you need to be very active in stimulating demand for your services or products.

This month it's very important to act according to your own conscience. When it comes to money, there are no quick fixes and easy solutions. Increasing your income and coping with financial issues is all about hard work, entrepreneurship and using your initiative. You should not resort to going into debt, using credit cards or applying for additional loans, it's better to go without or find ways to increase your income rather than to rely on other people, loans or debt.

Living and Loving to the Full

In August, physical touch is very important and that's why the way for you and your partner to ignite some romance and to improve things in the intimate sphere is by the introduction of sensuality and touch. This should not only include an increase in physical touch, giving each other hugs and massages etc., it should also involve using exotic oils with interesting fragrances, and perhaps interesting textures when it comes to the bed linen.

So maybe it's time to bring out the silk sheets or possibly if you prefer crisp Irish linen sheets, because these interesting textures and aromas can help improve the levels of arousal and excitement in the bedroom.

It's also good idea to excite each other by maybe running a feather over each other's body or if you fancy, and if it's not too extreme, using some honey or chocolate and licking it off each other.

Planetary Cautions

The Mercury retrograde period from the 24th creates some

instability within your finances which can mean added stress. Money management, budgeting and financial planning takes up a lot of your spare time and you may be stressed and a little distant. You may wish to diversify your investments and spread risk, it's a good time to talk about money. It's not advisable to take on added financial responsibility right now, so not a good time to raise questions about a major purchase.

Moon Magic

The new moon phase extends from the 16th of August to the 30th of August, this waxing phase is the perfect fortnight for new initiatives, setting plans, establishing goals, starting anything prospective and being proactive. This is the action phase, details below:

The waxing phase is great for recuperating and recharging batteries. New health and fitness activities or a change in image is successful. Brand name activities and competitive or entertainment activities are successful.

Psychic matters are favored. A good time for creative, music and artistic pursuits.

Great for socializing, parties and casual dating.

SEPTEMBER

Energies and Essence – "It's not the way I hoped or how I planned But somehow it's enough"

The essence and the energy is all about structure and creating security and stability in your life. It's very important to be organized and systematic in your thinking and planning and in business it's essential to develop strategies. However, in terms of your private life and your aims for yourself, it's also vital not to be haphazard, you want to be focused, to conserve energy and to ensure that you direct your aims in a way to have maximum chance of success.

This is not a time to disregard experience, you need to look back at how things worked out in the past and understand exactly why they were successful, or why they failed, and incorporate that information.

It's also vital to stick to your plans and to see things through to the end. This month the motto is winners don't quit and quitters don't win.

Remember, even if things don't work out exactly as you had planned, what's most important is that you develop the plan and you follow through, because something unexpected could also arise that will lead to a successful outcome.

Affirmation: "I appreciate all my experiences and I learn from them."

Love and Romance

This is definitely a great month for romantic communication, if you have been involved in any long-distance or cyber relationships where you're been chatting with someone, these can begin to get a lot more intense and the conversation may become more sexual.

Even in existing relationships, more spicy sexualized chat by text message, messenger or WhatsApp can serve to enhance the relationship right now, as well as to move it into a slightly more sexy phase.

Leo and new partner may lock horns, but this is an essential time of working out what each other's triggers are, understanding each other's sensitivities and working out what sort of humor or innuendo works and what the red flag areas are. So this can be a time of quite rapid learning in terms of new relationships, which can help improve understanding quickly.

Career and Aspiration

This is a good time for communicating with your client or customer base, and beginning to communicate information relevant to the end of the year or the holiday season. It's an excellent time for reviewing databases or email lists to see that all the information is up-to-date and relevant.

Communication is key to the viability of your business, and therefore you need to be sure that you are easy to contact and that you provide frequent feedback to clients and customers, especially via your social media sites.

Increasing your social media profile and maybe updating your LinkedIn or your professional profiles is key right now, as people may be looking for your skill set and how can they find you if you haven't updated your profile.

Adventure and Motivation

With Mars in Libra, this is a time when you enjoy meeting new people and taking spontaneous trips and journeys, these may be for work purposes or educational reasons.

A business trip or trip away to a seminar can be an exciting way to meet new people or new potential partners, and it can also create a little bit of a buzz and excitement in your life.

Arguing and debating your pet peeves or favorite topics on social media and Twitter can be quite a distraction for you, and while it may excite you and you will enjoy the intellectual conquests, on the other hand it could waste time.

You're quite easily drawn into arguments this month, some of these are unproductive and can represent tangents, so you should avoid these unless they have a purpose to fulfil.

This is a time of culmination; you can feel something is about to happen – something which will bring success and achievement but which still requires more work than you had anticipated. This can be a last minute dash to dot I's, cross T's to make sure things come to fruition as you anticipated.

You can resent anything that limits your freedom or scope of action, and yet you have to respect structures and limitations, and if someone offers a word of warning, listen! This is a time to pump the brakes rather than accelerate – you are in the mood to accelerate for sure, but hold back, the time is not ripe.

Marriage and Family

This is an excellent month for problem-solving and honest communication in relationships.

Venus is now direct in Leo which means there's an opportunity for you and a partner to gain renewed understanding to build bridges and to co-operate on important issues.

While you have strong views and want to express them, you're also very proactive and eager to address any issues which you have as a couple, or which you're facing together, with a conciliatory approach.

So this month you're capable of being tolerant and cooperative, but at the same time you're not passive and this creates a good basis for getting things done as a couple or working on your relationship through constructive conversation to iron out differences and improve understanding.

Money and Finance

Mercury goes direct on the 15th in Virgo meaning this is a much better time for investment and financial decisions. You may now have the information you need to create a clear strategy and understand exactly what to do next.

This is a good time for getting budgets done, looking at any recent quotes etc. because you'll have a much better idea of costs going forward.

Any accounting, tax organizing or financial administration should be done this month after Mercury goes direct, as you're very analytical and able to understand how all the various pieces of your financial puzzle fit together.

Living and Loving to the Full

This month Leo likes to feel spoilt and you want to feel special, it's important for Leo to feel appreciation and therefore to Living and Loving to the Full all it takes is some gifting, some thoughtfulness and a little additional warmth from your partner.

Key for this month is showing each other appreciation, striving for balance and working on trust.

It's very important to have quality time together to do things that you genuinely enjoy, because this enhances the relationship. All too often we find we are battling to keep our heads above water, and that means there is no time for a little bit of down time or fun in relationships.

It's an excellent month to organize a date night, to send the children off to their grandparents, their friends and just have time to do some fun things together. However, you should not over plan or over script, it's better to set aside the time and then to do something spontaneous together that you both feel in the mood for.

Planetary Cautions

With Jupiter now retrograde in Taurus, it's a time for a pause and reflect in terms of what you are doing in your career or aspirational development.

During this year you're made numerous new starts and you grabbed opportunities, but right now you need to consolidate, organize and understand exactly where you are and what you still need to do. If you grab any new opportunities right now you can end up with too much on your plate.

The key phrase at the moment is "too many cooks spoil the broth" so you want to avoid taking on too many different pieces of information or advice, too many new tasks, or possibly jumping into many different directions all at once. You need to understand what your core focus is and then double down on that, rather than seeking more new options.

Moon Magic

The new moon phase extends from the 14th of September to the 29th of September, this waxing phase is the perfect fortnight for new initiatives, setting plans, establishing goals, starting anything prospective and being proactive. This is the action phase, details below:

The waxing phase is not a great for highly competitive activities and public events. It's not suitable for a totally new venture. It's not ideal for leadership and decisiveness.

Short trips away and internet dating are successful. Good for romantic communication. Excellent for social activities and dating. Creative writing is successful. Good for website and marketing.

Good for new career directions and job interviews or promotion.

OCTOBER

***Energies and Essence – "With hunger at her heels
Freedom in her eyes"***

*The energy this month should be youthful and light, it's important for
you to be in touch with the eternal, free-spirited, youthful side of
yourself. As we go through life and its troubles, it's easy to become
jaded, cynical, negative and hard, as with age we tend to see more
problems than solutions simply because experience can make us a
little bit world-weary.*

*However, the challenge for you is to cast off the clothes, the scars
and the wrinkles of adulthood and recognize that part of you that is
forever young, and therefore hopeful, cheerful and filled with
wonder about the amazing opportunity that is life, and everything it
can offer.*

*Whatever we are, whoever we are and wherever we are in life,
there's always something to be cherished and appreciated and that
can bring a smile to our face, and that is what is important to focus
on this month.*

*Affirmation: "I embrace life with innocence and wonder as life is
precious and I chose to appreciate and notice little miracles every
day."*

Love and Romance

This can be a positive time in your love relations but can also be a
time when expectations have to be managed, it may be that you are a
little bit moody, as on one hand you feel exceptionally excited and
positive about your romantic life, and then you can swing to the
other extreme becoming extremely self-critical and creating

mountains out of molehills.

The important thing in love and romance is for you to find the middle ground. Whether you are single or in a new relationship, you have to seek a sense of balance and perspective, because it's all too easy for you to get carried away in a mode of thinking and to jump to conclusions.

Effective communication now means not making assumptions but rather listening clearly to what's being said, as I say you're way too eager to jump to conclusions rather than fully understanding what is going on and this can lead to problems.

Career and Aspiration

This month your mind is extremely strong, you have an immense amount of determination and while you can become fixated, you are also very good at following through on anything important. You will also use this month to employ positive thinking and affirmations as due to of a high degree of mental energy, which you are emitting, these have extra force.

This is an excellent time for public speaking and presentations where you either has to state your case, win a debate or compete against others to get the most attention.

Your words tend to have a lot of power right now, so you need to be very careful about how you use them. The motto right now is, "the word is more powerful than the sword" and therefore you can have a great influence on people, however you can also stir up a lot of opposition, and so you have to be careful about the way you use your powers of communication.

Adventure and Motivation

This month Leo gets a lot of satisfaction by setting yourself targets, particularly to do with physical fitness or dietary goals, and then achieving those targets.

This month is ideal for you learning new skills. So whether you want to learn a totally new sport or whether you want to really improve your golf swing, for example, or any other technique, this is a great month to do it and this can fill you with a sense of personal achievement.

Often this month you get an enormous boost from overcoming something, so overcoming an addiction or perhaps reaching a dietary goal by losing a certain amount of pounds, can leave you feeling on top of Old Smokey.

So while obsession can be a bad thing this month in terms of your relationships, it can serve as a very important way of focusing your mind on your health aims as well as sporting ambitions.

Marriage and Family

This is a very pragmatic time in marriage, responsibility tends to weigh heavily and sometimes there can be a slightly glass is half empty feeling. It's very important for Leo not to allow any negativity from your partner to affect yourself, it's important for you to detach from some of your partner's problems. So while you should show compassion, you should also avoid getting dragged into anything that is really your partner's issue to deal with.

It's important for Leo and your partner to be sensible and not to live in denial, but on the other hand it's also important that you don't allow her fears to have a hold over you and prevent you from doing things that feel instinctively right.

There may be a sense of inevitability right now, but you guys should not cave into that because you can still affect the outcome through effort and positive action.

Money and Finance

This month with Saturn retrograde moving into 0 degrees of Pisces, it is not a great time for refinancing or applying for a loan, and Leo should be cautious in all your dealings with government agencies.

This is not a good time for a joint venture, this is also not a good time for you to go into any financial agreement with complicated clauses and loads of obligations and restrictions.

Right now the way to generate money is through increasing effort, rather than juggling financial instruments or trying to reduce debt repayments.

While there can be setbacks this month, the important thing is not to let it slow your momentum. You have to keep a positive, forward looking attitude and this will help you to tackle problems and still to keep moving forward. The last thing you should do is give up or take a step back and let things get you down.

The key to success is establishing and maintaining a positive mindset. Also key is to align with people who have an idealistic attitude, because as you make your way through this month it's important to ally with others who encourage you, who don't overwhelm or stifle you and who will give you a lot of support encouragement or even good advice.

Living and Loving to the Full

This month signals the potential for more excitement and passion in love; things are heating up for Leo emotionally. Your relationship is likely to take on a very sensual and mystical character this month, and the same holds true of potential romances if you're single.

You and your partner need to work on flirtation and demonstrating attraction and admiration of each other physically.

However, there's a deeper side to this month in terms of spiritual understanding. If you're been with a partner for a significant period, and the passion has faded, now is the opportunity to revive that again and rekindle the flames by having deep and meaningful conversations which make you guys feel more emotionally connected.

Planetary Cautions

This month it's important for Leo to avoid becoming obsessive, sometimes you get a bee in your bonnet and you just can't let something go, and you can take offence very easily or you can overreact to small things.

Leo need to be more cognizant of where these obsessive extreme reactions come from at a psychologist level and you may need to reflect a little bit on the underlying issues that are making you so easily triggered this month.

It might be a good time for you to avoid any situation that would cause you to be criticized or demeaned in anyway by others, it's probably not a good idea to try humor in the workplace or relationships because this can backfire.

Moon Magic

The new moon phase extends from the 14th of October to the 30th of October, this waxing phase is the perfect fortnight for new initiatives, setting plans, establishing goals, starting anything prospective and being proactive. This is the action phase, details below:

The waxing phase is not a great for emotional confrontation or discussion. You're very subjective and partial, so this is not a good time for clear-headed decision making as you're very excitable and quite extreme.

Good for marriage and engagement. Excellent for date nights. Good for marriage counselling.

Essence and Energies – "Solid, solid as a rock."

The essence this month is building on solid foundations. We all know that a house divided cannot stand and that a building with weak foundations also cannot stand, so these are two things to bear in mind as you go about your life.

So what I'm saying is, it's very important to try and encourage cooperation or to pour oil over troubled waters when it comes to matters within your own family. Remember, we are all stronger when we have a supportive family unit behind us and sometimes it can take work to create that, so often working on family relationships is an investment that will put you in good stead in the future.

In terms of any career or personal goals, it's important to put in the groundwork and also lay a solid foundation in terms of planning and investment. So if there's something that you are very keen to achieve, make sure that from the get go everything is in place and nothing is neglected, as a small crack in the foundations can trip you up later.

Affirmation: "I understand what's most important to my success and well-being and I resolve to build strength into my relationships and the structures in my life."

Love and Romance

This is an excellent time for romantic self-expression, communication in love relationships improves and suddenly things seem to click and you might feel like you are finally on the same wavelength as a new partner.

This month is very important for increasing understanding in new relationships, so again it's vital for Leo to say what's on your mind and to express effectively where you stand on certain matters.

It could be a time in new relationships when you guys start talking about children and whether to have them, or if it's later in life, it could be a time where you both let your children know about your relationship, or start incorporating them into activities that you guys are doing. So the whole family get to know one another better this month, because this is also an important family time as well as a romantic bonding time.

Career and Aspiration

During this time you can feel a little bit drained, it's often the case that you run out of steam in terms of your desire to do things in public, do PR or do social media marketing.

So this may be a good month to avoid anything particularly demanding in terms of corporate entertaining, lecturing or publicity and spend more time doing research or analyzing data.

This can be an excellent time for conducting market research and using that to help clarify the decisions that you're going to be making next year.

If Leo is working from home this may be a very important month to get organized and more streamlined, so that the activities that you are doing for your work within the home environment do not impinge on the needs or lifestyles of other family members. Thus work life balance is important, but what is also important is harmonizing your home office with the requirements of the rest of the family.

Adventure and Motivation

This is the time when Leo should get in touch with your inner child, and that involves being spontaneous and doing things that make you feel young again. This can be an excellent time to participate in sports or coaching with young people because their youthful enthusiasm rings a bell with you, and awakens inside of yourself that which may have been dormant.

You may get a kick out of playing pranks, you're certainly a joker this month and you like to surprise others and use your wit to provoke a reaction or inspire laughs.

You have to remember to be sensitive, but usually whether you use your humor to tell jokes or to clown around, it helps and lighten the mood.

Marriage and Family

This month there are two themes running through all relationships: one is to do with sharing and making financial decisions together, and this can affect both very new and existing relationships, simply because doing things together involves spending money and one has to negotiate how that's going to happen. It's important to show compassion and also cooperation when it comes to money, you should not ignore issues if you feel that your partner should be contributing more and is not pulling their weight. It's time for you to address that, but at the same time if you feel that your partner is wanting to live a life beyond your particular means (e.g. if you are dating) it's very important for you not to be shy to say that.

The second element is sex and intimacy. This is a time win sex life can become extremely rewarding and the intimate sphere of your relationship can take off, but strong intimacy starts with strong boundaries. So often saying NO and telling your partner where your red lines and limits are in terms of the bedroom, can actually be a gateway to better understanding. Thus if you feel reticent about talking to a partner about what you do or don't like, because having those conversations can actually be a gateway to for better communication, to respect developing and the relationship becomes a lot secure and more secure because you both know where you stand.

So the key to relationships this month is to tackle the grey areas, financially and sexually, and make sure you both know exactly where you stand. Mean what you say and say what you mean.

Money and Finance

This maybe a month when Leo has to shell out on things to do with repairs or renovations connected to the home. It's important for you to ensure that all insurance is up to date, and it may also be necessary to spend more money on securing your property.

Anything you have neglected to take care of in terms of money will crop up now, and suddenly become urgent. So you can't kick the can down the road, this is a time to deal with problems decisively.

This is definitely the time to plug any gaps or leaks, so if you are spending money or wasting money on any activity or business cost that isn't vitally necessary, that has to go. Some pruning of outgoings may be required.

Living and Loving to the Full

This month emotions are more complicated and raw, which can lead to some misunderstandings or even manipulation and concealment, not everything is as it appears.

Leo must put effort into getting to the bottom of things, and you must uncover the intentions of others in your family, but also understand better your own emotions and how they inadvertently impact on others.

Old attitudes, beliefs or ideas which could be clouding your judgement have to be reviewed, as things that are hiding in your unconscious are affecting your ability to accept love.

Past relationships that may be haunting you, or a loss of faith in love as a concept must be tackled as these can have profound effects on how you approaches relationships.

Planetary Cautions

This is a month to avoid having house guests, visitors or entertaining within the home. This is not a good time to invite the in-laws to stay or host any parties because they can end up being more trouble than they are worth.

This is definitely a time for moderation, Leo is very impetuous and you tend to jump into activities without thinking them through. This is a very important month to avoid damage escalation, often wading into something and taking a sledgehammer to crack a nut can only create more problems and more frustration, so you have to be measured in your response to any problems.

Moon Magic

The new moon phase extends from the 13th of November to the 27th of November, this waxing phase is the perfect fortnight for new initiatives, setting plans, establishing goals, starting anything prospective and being proactive. This is the action phase, details below:

The waxing phase is not a great time for marriage, engagement or solidifying a relationship. Negotiation and new business partnerships aren't favored.

Brand new activities and risky ventures aren't successful. It's not a good waxing period for extreme sports or very physically demanding work. Performance and musical pursuits aren't successful.

This isn't a great time for retreats or humanitarian aims.

Personal financial analysis and investment is successful. A good time for investment in jewelry and metals.

Career and business expansion goals are successful, but leadership or entrepreneurship is not necessarily favored.

DECEMBER

Essence and Energies – "I'm a shooting star leaping through the sky like a tiger
Defying the laws of gravity"

There's a very assertive energy about this month, you can get things done. If you pick a task or set a goal, you should achieve it without much opposition as you have the wind in your sails. It's easy to be courageous and if you sense an opportunity, run with it. You can win in both sporting competitions or where intellectual ability is needed.

You work hard and play hard, you are not in a self-denying mood at all, you have a zest for all aspects of life from work to pleasure. It's important to you to achieve right now, and in that regard you take more risks, you have a strong sense that no matter how things pan out, your determination and energy can steer those events to a victory at the end. You are in quite a rebellious phase and can be controversial. You have a great deal of love in your heart, but you tend to express it universally rather than personally.

Affirmation: "My zest for life fuels me and ignites my creativity. I radiate positivity in my relationships."

Love and Romance

Leo is very demanding in your new relationships, you are quite impulsive and you tend to want to express yourself freely, so you're not always very understanding because you are far more focused on instant gratification and also have very low impulse control. So if there's something you want, you're determined to get it and unfortunately if you don't get your own way you can become quite stroppy.

However you're a lot of fun to be around and have a huge zest for life this month, so if you guys are generally agreed on what to do, you can have a lot of fun and also generate a lot of warmth and affection, but if you have differences about how to spend your time and what you enjoy doing, then it's probably best for you guys to go your separate ways, enjoy yourselves in your own unique ways and come together only where appropriate.

Leo is not always particularly sympathetic with a partner who's depressed, feels more tired or introverted this month, you're not into to delaying your own gratification, and so you either are up for it or you aren't going to hang around waiting for you to get in the mood.

Career and Aspiration

You tend to throw your heart and soul into the various creative pursuits that you enjoy right now and they can be very successful.

Business and professional activities connected to children may become more prevalent in your life, you may find during phase you deal with children in various capacities, and this can help awaken the inner child and bring a part of you alive.

While you have to work harder in your communications with others, you can achieve significant results. It may be that you have more difficulty communicating with your coworkers, you superiors or maybe things between you and certain clients are strained. Generally you have to be careful with the way you communicate, you have to be deliberate, but you should also be succinct. So it's certainly is a time when you learn new communication skills that will possibly be effective in the future.

Adventure and Motivation

Leadership and publicity orientated activities are perfect for Leo guy. It's an excellent time for you as you can have a lot of fun and excitement by hosting parties, by arranging the entertainment in some respect when it comes to the Christmas party or being the entertainment yourself.

This is a very successful and fulfilling time for those Leo who work in a career that involves sports, entertainment or creating fun and excitement for people because you should get excellent feedback and that encouragement will spur you on.

You love to be in control and you love the limelight, so any role where you can take the lead, make the decisions and use your own creativity and unique spark will certainly appeal to you.

Marriage and Family

This month, sex and physical love making is more important to Leo and thus it's important for your partner to be sexually expressive and you guys to make your sex life more exciting with maybe some new tricks, toys and costumes to create a bit of pizzazz in the bedroom.

This is a much better month for entertaining and you guys may enjoy having mutual friends over for cocktail parties or events, and often having people in the home helps you both to feel more amorous. It's probably going to help more if your guests are your peers as you guys may not feel as amorous if the guests are one of your respective parents.

You guys may enjoy shopping together, particularly for items for the home, which will enhance both your lives over the Christmas period and beyond. This is a good time to make a considered purchase for the improvement of your home.

Money

It's best for you to get your ducks in a row as far as money goes before the 13th of the month when Mercury goes retrograde in Capricorn.

Before the 13th is an excellent time for you to organize your finances, use any new technology to help you with accounting or to outsource any bookkeeping tasks in order for more speed or efficiency to be achieved.

The first fortnight of the month is also good for improving cash flow, investing and activities in the service sector are particularly profitable.

Things tend to slow down a lot from the middle of the month as many people will be taking time off early for Christmas, and that's why the bulk of your economic activity must be packed into the first two weeks.

Living and Loving to the Full

This December you can enhance your love life with date nights and novel activities that encourage the adrenaline to flow.

So adventure and action films, exciting sports events, theme parks, concerts or dancing is an excellent way to get you both revved up and in the mood for passion in the bedroom. You want to feel alive and often adrenaline packed activities really put the spark back and can be enormously useful emotionally or sexually.

Depending on your budget or tastes, motor bike riding, white river rafting, skiing or any thrilling activity helps get the love juice pumping again. So whatever you guys decide to do, don't be bland, be outrageous.

Planetary Cautions

During this month you will lack discipline in doing the things that you really don't want to do, so if there are any tasks which are unappealing, hard to get into or really bore you, there's absolutely no point in you pursuing those this month, as you will simply get frustrated or end up doing a bad job.

December may not be the best month for decisions about children, it can be difficult to discipline children and come to understandings with them, so it's probably a good month to have a laissez faire attitude towards the children, and wait until another time to reign them in, or if they are adults, have those more tricky conversations with them.

Moon Magic

The new moon phase extends from the 12th of December to the 26th of December, this waxing phase is the perfect fortnight for new initiatives, setting plans, establishing goals, starting anything prospective and being proactive. This is the action phase, details below:

The waxing phase is a great time for new relationships and romance. Date nights, short romantic getaways, romantic communication and cyber dating is all favored.

Sports, competitive activities and entertainment pursuits are favored.

Corporate events and social entertaining are successful.

Excellent for negotiation, conciliation and reconciliation.

Sales and marketing are successful. An excellent time for a promotion or job interviews. New business opportunities can be grabbed.

You need to be careful of your health and to eat well. Mercury going retrograde in Capricorn on the 14th is not ideal for diets, medical procedures, dentistry or new exercise routines.

Work with animals isn't favored. Not a good time for office romance.

Wrapping Up

Well that's a wrap of my biggest most comprehensive Leo Horoscope yet.

Whether you are a Leo or know a Leo, I do believe you will have found this very helpful and informative.

I aim to give you a variety of advice based on psychology, spiritual insight, relationship advice and business guidance, so you get a little bit of everything.

Take care and have a wonderful 2023.

Blessings, Lisa.

Made in the USA
Middletown, DE
10 April 2023

28549393R00061